Making Love With Words                Cathy BLUE

Original Name: Making Love With Words
Original Language: English

Copyright © Tülay ASLAN. 2021

First edition, July 2021

Book design by Tülay ASLAN
Cover Photo by Tülay ASLAN

ISBN 978-625-00-9785-4

Published by Tülay ASLAN

Index

# Making Out With Words

We write for the one,
Well-knowing these words
We bled out in ink
Will never be read by them.


May be it is the beauty of it,
There is nothing now
Holding us back to use our words,
No fear of losing,
What we already do not have.


I am not afraid,
I am wide-open to the possibility.
As I will wait,
I am making out with words,
Daydreaming your lips.


Love,

Cathy

# Lost In A Fantasy

Our bodies sated and spent,
Our limbs entwined,
You kiss me slowly.
If you are a dream,
Why can't you be true?
How am I left
So satisfied
To my core?

# BitterSweet

*"She's both heaven and hell,"*
All wrapped together,
In a shiny blue package,
A golden ribbon.


Taste me baby,
I'll melt in your mouth.


I'm both heaven and hell,
Bittersweet on your tongue.

# Marriage

 I am standing forsaken at the precipice,
Clenching this feeble hope in my heart
Whether to push you down
Or jump myself.
The waves beneath our feet,
Tempting sirens, restless,
Are calling your name.

# Watching You

Watching you line kisses
To my back,
Our gazes meet in the mirror,
A confident smirk is all I get.
A wide smile on my face
Turns to a gasp then a throaty moan,
When you whisper my name
To my neck.

# The Siege

Our gazes meet over
the campfire,
Your hands still on your sword,
My hands still on my sword,
We share a quiet moment,
Stolen from the deaths of others.
You lift your chin up in acknowledge,
I lower my head slowly,
Hiding the smile threatening to bloom.


*Your wish is my command, my commander.*

# Making A New Nest

*-This is for a family member, D&A,*
*all the love and best wishes of the universe for you-*

The first time I held you
In my arms, cradling you,
I promised you, you are loved.


All the years we had,
I watched you
Become the amazing man
You have become.


Trying to be your own person,
Finding your way
Through the challenges of life.
Look baby boy,
How far you have come.


Building of your own family,
Every bird needs to fly
To make their own cozy nest.
Happy tears on my face.

The waves of the ocean
Washes away the worries,
You are loved,
It whispers to all lovers.


Like the ocean, surrounding the world,
I will always be there,
You are loved,
forever and always.

# Second Language

They tried to eavesdrop,
Hearing nothing in our silent dialogue.
You gave me a wicked smile,
I grinned at you like the lovesick fool I am.
It was a conversation of stars,
Our hearts spoke,
Our eyes approved.
They heard nothing.

# My Vow (V1/V2/V3)

From your very first breath,
Till the last,
You are loved.


The serene sound of the waves,
Washing the shores,
The melody of the chirping birds
We embrace each other,
We make a promise,
In good and bad,
You are loved,
You are gonna be loved,
Forever and always.


In every breath I take,
In every small smile you get,
From your very first breathe,
You have been loved.


In each and every day,
Not just a mother's or sister's,
Now also a wife's heart

Making Love With Words          Cathy BLUE



You have.
You are loved,
Forever and always.


Loved you are,
Deeply like an ocean
Surrounding the world
In a mother's cradle..


Loved you are,
Passionately like a flame,
Reaching the sky.


In every breath you inhale,
You are loved,
Forever and always.

# Sing Me A Song

I knew it from the start,
Our love never had a happy ending
Just like our hollow song.

# Medallion

I wear all my scars
Like the Medallions of war.
Except one,
You are my cherished scar,
I hid you away in my heart
From their prying eyes.

# Tiger

You hold on
To the crumble of love
You see in a tiger's eyes.


You put your hand in mine,
Watching me lick my fur clean.
I roar but we both know
I had always held your heart,
Gracefully in my paws.

# Ghost paint

Salty tears of mine
Like these paintings
On my wall
Painted in ghost dye.
Only then
They will glow in dark
Trying to light up
The pitch black.

# Deep

From hell to this realm
I had made it so far
In one piece, mostly intact.
I have been looking for a shelter,
To lower my guard,
Can I travel to your heart?
Are you at home?
Will you answer the door?
Will you pretend to be out?

# Cursed

Our love will remain unseen
And untouched will my body be.
This moment, we share,
Will be just another story
In a damned fairytale.

# PassionART

My body is a blank canvas,
Paint me in the fierce colors of your passion,
Draw me in, draw me out,
Fill me in,
Print your hands and mouth
All over me.

# Death Of Me

We sat together,
Under the stars.
We drank and drank,
Laughing at the odds
Of us to be together.


I died a little inside,
Drank a little more.
Dead can not weep.
My tears I heap.

# Ecstasy

The satin sheets I clutch,
This pleasure is too much,
Everywhere burns when you touch,
You are guzzling down your punch.


The blood in my veins is in a rush,
All my body becomes a pink flush,
You put a hand to my mouth, *HUSH!*
I fall apart and into the bed, I crush.

# Flirting?

I grow, I know,
I glow, my words flow.


Is it love?
It fits like a glove,
In every shove.

# Veil

Color me black
The darkness sucks me in deep.
On and off, you talk about
The sparkles, glitters,
Black is the color
Of my dreams,
Watching the world
Pass by behind a mourning veil.

# Rain Lover

The rain speaks to my soul,
*"Get a cup of tea,*
*Lean back darlin'.*
*For once,*
*I will sing you*
*A lullaby."*

# Dream-Chaser

I am tired of chasing after you,
Like a cat in heat, you climb the roof,
Gotta fetch a ladder and take you down.
You run and hide in my closet
Like all the skeletons I bury deep.
The moment my hand reaches
For the knob,
There you go, running again.
Curses line behind my lips,
I swallow them back and chase,
Chase after what I can never have.
*"Gotchaaaaaa,"* I manage to say,
It slips down the rain.
Rip.

# Abyss

The longing makes me wanna fly to you,
Gravity keeps my soul anchored
To this human body,
I stand still in the abyss in-between.

# Windy

Your kisses linger on my lips,
Your husky whispers inside my mind,
I embrace the void already
Before the wind blows again.

# Stress-Eater

You are like
A handful of chocolate chips
I consume, *"stress-eating"* they say.
*"Guilty pleasures,"* I correct.
Not good for the body
But oh boy,
Does it pump dopamine
To the soul?


*Shh, we all know*
*It is always more than a handful*
*I consume.*

# Paranoia

Grabbing the cup of tea in my hand,
I watch the kids play and think,
If tomorrow starts without me,
Will anyone love them
The way I do?
Paranoia and worry etches my face,
I hide my fall behind the cup,
Take a sip, take a breath, carry on.

# Forest Fae

I danced, removed my skin off,
*-It always fit too tight-*
I danced more,
Bared my soul to sycamore.
Its shadow kept me unseen,
The rustle of leaves kept me unheard,
We snuggled,
Its seeds on my skin,
Gave me the wings.
Now I fly high,
Leaving the trail of our sins.

# Story Of The Lark

The sky pours down on the lark,
With nowhere to hide,
It crashes down to the earth,
Wings broken, barely alive.
The wind blows fiercely,
Covers the lark with dry leaves.
*"Sleep well little one,*
*I will sing you a lullaby,*
*Mummy will keep you safe and warm."*

# Fallen Angel

Our hearts are traitors to our own existence,
Little sardonic bastards they are,
Leading us here and there by the leash.


One day, me and myself,
We got tired of this shit,
You know, being dragged down,
Dragged all around by the leash.
We made plans,
Booked a tropical holiday in Guatemala,
To see Fuego Volcano.


Erupted the volcano,
Covered everywhere in cums of molten lava,
We tried to run, slipped and fell.
*RUPTURE!*
Did we hear a scream?


We left a bait to lavas,
A not-so-virgin offering to the Fuego,
Me and myself, hand in hand,
Walked back home, numb.

# Snapshot

A cup of hot tea,
Sitting on my desk,
Vapor of it is a dancing siren
To the beat inside my head.
One of these silent nights,
I am glad to be alive,
Writing my heart out.

# Mistletoe

I have never been very good
At mathematics,
But if I have to make a quick calculation,
It is almost %0.00000001,
For us to stand together
Under a mistletoe,
Notice it and share a kiss,
Laughing at the absurdity.

# Ouch

You ask me when was
The last time
We made love.
I say *"It was long ago,"*
*"It was yesterday,"* you say
At the same time.
We fall into a very disturbing silence now.

# Playing Hard-To-Get

Sleep runs, I follow it,
It likes to play coy,
Marking me as the hunteress.
Watching ceiling for hours, with dusk,
It finally lulls me into my dark numbness.

# Not Really

This fed up twist of my lips
Is your crescent moon,
It does not light up your sky,
You claim.

# Tender Night

The night falls upon us,
I can finally breathe in relief.
She says,
*"Rest, take a break to tend your wounds,*
*I will tuck you in,*
*My sweet moon child."*

# A Fall I Will Love

Pumpkin pie tastes your kiss, a little tinted pumpkin
spice coffee,
The orange, red leaves of the fall are under our boots.
You stare at me, our souls embrace each other in silence.

# Fairytale

They asked me to write for a tale in 18 words,
All i could think:
*It is over.*

# Love For Summer

Crazy mid-summer sun, all you do is scorch,
RIP my now lobster skin! I touch and OUCH!

# Crafting

Glitter and glue, glitter and glue,
Colorful pom poms here and there,
I wish we could craft out
My life from the beginning
Just like that.

# Fun fact

*"You write so beautiful and raw."*
Yes I know,
The wound is open and ugly,
I am still
Bleeding all over
Because of one-sided love.

# What Am I?

What am I,
An angel in disguise?
A devil in disguise?
They gave me fluffy wings
That dragged me down to hell.
They gave me a halo,
A crown fit for a fallen.
They scorched my skin,
Made their own tattoos,
A pat on my back
And a long tail for my bravery,
I use it as a whip.
Not a real angel,
Not a real devil.
Oh baby,
What am I?

# Tipsy

A lil' tipsy from the champagne,
Now I will admit.
I have a high-school crush at you,
No day passes without hearing your voice
This way or another.


Your voice carries me to the beach
Where the wild waves do not drag me down,
You keep me sane.


I go star-struck
Every time
I hear
Your voice.

# High

I will not be responsible for anything
I say or write after that point,
I dream of you, in front of me, *KNEEL!*
You look like my favorite meal,
All these fancy clothes, one by one, I peel,
I feel your lips over mine, feels so surreal.
I am so high, I repeat, it is all unreal,
This steamy exchange, it is so surreal.

# Flirting With Words

You are a wound that will not heal,
All I have is an itch, it feels so real
I try but i can not, you are all I feel
All these logical rules, none appeal,
Baring my soul,my love, I wanna reveal,
SHIT! You are now as hard as steel.

# Celebrating On My Own

I love you without a break,
The same way I consume
My poison of choice.
I look back to my desk,
Half-full / Half-empty
Sits my champagne bottle.
Seems like I will
Have a hangover anyways,
*-Over a bottle of champagne?*
*One-sided love?*
*These words that will not leave,*
*GODDAMN!-*
Now, as well,
Finish the rest of the bottle.

# Chaos

The more I drink,
The more emotions I get.
How is that even possible?
The alcohol, isn't it supposed to numb the feelings?
I just choke up
On my emotions now.
Like a sand storm,
Pain, hurt, fear,
Circles me all around,
Until i hold my knees,
Rock myself back and forth
And cry,
Typing through blurry eyes,
In front of my laptop.

# Crisis

I caught myself
Crying, telling a perfect stranger
About my emotional status,
I question myself, darlin,
What on earth
Am I doing?????

# Propose

Over and over I think
In my drunken state
And when high as the universe.
Try i might,
With all I might
I had never seen
A lifetime
We were not
Together.


Maybe we reached
The chapter of our story
Where boy
Notices the girl,
Falls,
Falls down,
Down to
His knees.

# Patience

Like all these heartaches
That chokes us down
On our own salvia,
This pain one day
Will subside.
Patience my heart,
Patience.

# Enlightenment

Wow, I had just entered a new level of drinking game:
Am I drinking for all the things we had lost?
Am I drinking for all the things we could be together?
Shit, I feel too wasted for that level,
Need to sit down and think for a while for this level.
My brain is highly intoxicated to think of anything
But you, your voice, your hands all night long.

# All These Endless Questions

The sobriety hits me up hard
I wanna crawl in bed, retch.
A so utopical dream I chase,
If I have the guts to tell you,
You would laugh all night long.
I, I do not know what I am doing here,
But I stand in the abyss,
Ready to take the leap of faith,
Fly to what I dream.
Makes me think and question,
How wrecked in the head I am?

# Cold Tiles On My Face

I feel sick down to my stomach,
Not sure if it is the poison of my choice
Or the emotions that accompanied as well.


I want to hug my knees,
Press my forehead to cold tiles,
Throw up
Whatever is left of us,
Dream or reality.

# Self-Heal

Writing without roaring,
Writing my inner monologue,
Sometimes, not always,
It helps a lot
For my self-healing.
These tender words
I bleed out,
Tend out to
All ugly, open
Wounds I have.

# Glitter Glue

I am breaking down,
I am breaking apart
One word at a time.
I question,
What glues me together?

# Doubts

Tears of mine,
Dried on their own
When they noticed
They had nowhere to go
But deep down
My heart,
My silence of death,
Where they belong.
Where do I belong???

# Divorce

That night when I came downstairs in tears
And asked you If you loved me the way you used to.
The shock on your face and the denial
You swallowed back in a second
Told me all  I needed to know.


I cried it out of my chest, I slept it over.
Now I am only moving ahead,
Not numb, but with gratitude,
Knowing it is all over
So I am free,
So are you?

# Withering

All these words on the pale pages,
Fallen petals of a once in full blossom rose,
Gives withering to all readers.
A lost love.
Let's celebrate!

# Period

You come and go as you please,
Never caring of what I feel,
Never giving me a chance to brace.
Heartbreaks all over, unexpected visitor.

# Woman Behind The Mask

I tug it down little,
Nudge to left,
Swipe to the right an inch.
Now, fits perfect
On my face,
Flashing a megawatt smile,
Cute dimples to the onlookers,
It clogs everything else,
Heartbreak of mine,
Tears of anger,
All cloaked barriers
Behind the mask I wear
Every single day.

# 2 Souls As 1

*-This collab with m'twin, Em, leaving my*
*heart here as well-*

*''You held your heart from me*
*like a cloaked barrier.*
*So long now I'm just a bulldozer*
*looking to escape.''*


All the world, all the universe,
I could have given to you,
My heart I can not,
This piece, can't bear to lose.


*"Why do you hide what used to be?*
*The real you, the real me.*
*Once I thought the mystery drew like the mist.*
*Now the mist is all I see.''*


All these tiny drops of tears
All over my frayed skin,
I stay still,
Heart loaded with questions

Of endless possibilities.


*"Unknown and bewildered*
*Clutching at splintery straws*
*Which way is up, which do I choose?*
*How much will be to lose?"*


Losing myself and finding you?
Finding you or losing myself?
This coffin of love
Feels too small
Even for a dove.


*"Oh great tsunami free me from this cloaked barrier*
*Release this unsurmounting  pressure in my chest*
*Leaden jacket*
*Can't breathe*
*Whispered lies and lullabies."*


Not playing hard-to-get,
My favourite has always been deaf-mute-blind.
The intensity of this firework emotions,
Explosion over explosion inside our chests,
I do not think we will make it

Alive,
Out of this love.

# Twinkle

I had always looked up to you
To make it out of this ocean of despair,
To find my way back home,
The determined sailor I was.


My little star,
Sitting so bright
In its own bouquet of constellations.
Lead the way home,
My heart, my soul.
UNITE!

# Can You Rhyme The Pain Out?

A little here, a bit there, piece by piece
One tear at a time, I release.
The pain does not decrease,
I want some inner peace,
The intensity of living, on increase.


Chin up, hold your head high,
This shall be our last goodbye.
My tears will soon dry,
I won't ask again why.


Every time you touch, I die.
I am now a cloudless, gray sky,
Dull and hollow to the eye.
No birds can fly so high.
Now, this is my last goodbye.

# Sinking

Asphyxiated,
Feather light my body,
The heavy burden of a cold heart I carry,
We sink deep down in the darkness of the sea.
Time is now disoriented over my skin,
My conscious is shattered,
Still it stays there,
Your handprints on my heart,
In your attempt to rip it out.

# Earthquake

Your lips, your hands, your husky voice,
I welcome all, arms wide open,
Knowing what a catastrophe we will be.

# Sing Me Out

I am a song and I need you to sing me out.
I am written in tears, raw pain and brutal honesty,
I am muted on white paper, I stay still and wait.


I am a song and I need you to sing me out,
Be a voice to my pain and I will be your echo,
Together, we can take down this world,
Just sing me out, my words, your voice.
We can be one, forever together.

# Demand On Paper

I want to erase all the memories of others
Who touched you before me.
You washed your skin clean,
That spicy scent of yours is my downfall.
I wanna rhyme your soul out,
Turn you inside out,
Cut open and stitch alive,
For my sheer pleasure,
I want to rhyme on your skin
In my hoarsely whispered words,
I want to breathe you in,
Take you all the way down.
I want you make you lovesick,
A king for a strong queen.

# Lucid Dreaming

Your husky voice echoes inside me,
The woooosh of the blood in my veins,
The erratic breathing of us.


You bury yourself  deep in me, I swear I see stars,
It is nothing compared to what I am feeling,
Just a hollow dream to cut me open
Every time.

# Hoping, Hoping

I breathe, look up to the sky, smile,
Still there is a tiny possibility for us,
Hope rising in my chest.

# Bleeding Out

I want to break your spell over me,
This thin hope I'm holding onto
Is gonna anchor me down to my fall.
I am crying out my heart in papers, in agony.

# Starry Night

Restless and all hyperactive,
These giddy stars in me
Come out in bed time
To play hide and seek
In your pitch black sky.
Are you ready to be dazzled?

# Heated

Phosphenes dance in front of my eyes,
You grip my chin, lay open-mouthed kisses on my jaw.
I try to form some words in the back of my throat,
*"Deeper,"* is all I manage in an animalistic roar.

# Love Language

We sat in a comfortable silence, for a time,
Then smiled at each other,
Well knowing the secret crush we both shared.
No words were exchanged,
Magically, it was enough...for now.

# Starry Eyed

I am always starstruck around you.
Your eyes are elixir gemstones to my soul,
They always sparkle funky rainbows meeting my gaze.

# Undisclosed

I had always been drawn
To whiskey voice,
Deeper it gets,
More shivers I get.
Your voice?
Gives me dancing butterflies,
Trying to break out of my skin.
With love, always.

# Sorry :(

You crushed
Petals of my heart
In your harsh grip.
Sorry,
No glue fixes that.

# Night Breeze

I lay with the window open wide,
I kick the covers down,
Let the night breeze
Caress my skin in feather light touches,
Fill me in,
Chill my overheated skin.

# Facts Are Facts

All the best stories I came across here and there,
None had a happy ending.
I repeat this fact to my wrecked heart.

# Eternal

Your voice has always been
An endless echo
In the hectic maze of my mind.
You buried yourself
Deep and deeper
Into my soul.
Now I lick my own skin
To get another taste of you.

# Phantom Lover

Show me some love tonight,
Be the mist to my world.
From head to toe,
Every freaking inch of mine,
Cover with yours.

# The Riot

That emotions I have bottle up
Inside my fragile human body
Are starting a riot,
That cunning and deceitful hope,
That misguided expectation,
That foolish love I carry.


Cement and mortar,
I build up more and more
Walls for the castle
To keep them deep down,
To protect the sanity of my consciousness.

# Love Of A Poet

Slide in me,
Deep down to the hilt,
Eye to eye,
Chest to chest,
Heart to heart,
Define me
With your words.
Let my body be your paper,
Yours a pen,
Write us out
Until we are both full
With words.

# Dimples

Watching you nervously chuckle
Then smile in embarrassment,
Lick these lips I wanna kiss….
*Oh boy, oh boy,*
*I am so glad you have no idea*
*About the train of my thoughts.*
I smile my dimples out back to you,
Wanna kiss me on my dimples?

# Talk

I swoon over the songs of past,
They always carry your husky voice.
Babe, would you like to
Talk my ear off or
Whisper the sh*t out of it?
I am open to both possibilities.

# Sunset

You are the sunset of my soul
Leaving pinkish-reddish-purplish
Stains all over my soul.
I embrace sunset, farewell sun.


A pinkish purple sunset,
I watched myself bleed all over.
It felt surreal and heartbreakingly beautiful.
I offered myself a sad smile, moved on.

# MEOW

You have the power over me
*-To which I will never submit-*
Yet, you hold the power over me
To make me purr, hiss and MEOW
Like a cat in the heat.
*MEOW!*

# RibCage

I tried to make it fit,
Take it all the way down.
It tried to stretch all my walls,
Broke down some.
This pain we carry
Will never fit inside our ribcage.
Yet, onlookers claim
*The universe is expanding.*
We shall see...

# Just A Random Thought

Warm westerlies slap me in the face,
It is like summer saying *muhahaha,*
*Suck it up, I'm still here bitch.*

# Silly Girl

Hold me gently,
Because I crumble under
The heavy pressure
Of this burden of love
I carry.


Hold me gently,
I am too proud
To fall apart
Yet too naive
To believe
I will make my way
Out of this love
Alive.

# Diamonds Are A Girl's Best Friend

Can't escape these lucid daydreams of memories.
Mind is on repeat mode,
Playing your cold words,
Dividing my consciousness
Into tiny diamonds of heartbreaks.

# NOXIOUS

I wanna get high on my own blood,
This restless itching messes with my mind.
Itch, be the first one to draw blood,
Rip your skin off,
A new layer will form
Without knowing the touch of your noxious kisses.

# Charm Bracelets

These scars we all carry
Are our charms, fearless charms.
They add unique arts to our body
Proving that we had survived,
We are surviving,
We will survive and not bow
To the cruelty of this joke of the world.

# Idea

They got it all wrong,
I am not in love with you,
But with the idea of you
Inside my own head.

# Talking With My Heart

Take the hit my heart,
We had asked for it
When you had decided to
Chase after an impossible love.


All my warnings, pleads
Fell on your deaf ears.
Now you fall apart,
Bleed us both out.


I will hold you safe,
These hits we took together
In the name of freaking love
Will never kill you and me.


*Between us girls,*
*I do not think*
*We will come back*
*From that one either.*

# Hatred

*"Someone had too much drinks…"*
Comes the sinister comment,
*"Again,"* adds more to the fire.
In the dark hallway, I glare
Without words.
The hatred in my eyes has
Always been your choice of poison.
I leave you there, standing in the dark,
Always judging, always belittling.
I stagger with the weight of my own heartbreak,
I stagger to my bed, to my home,
I stagger with the weight of knowing
This is not even the end.

# Death

The days are counted,
Beat by beat,
Second by second,
My heart is waiting
For the day
To fly out of this rusted cage
Called Life/Love.

# Surviving The Silence

I swallow everything back down,
They go down my throat,
Sprinkles of glass, handfuls.
The words, my heartfelt words,
The words are dead
In my mouth,
My heart dies a little more,
Nothing I can not handle.

# Night Of A Poetess

Stab, stab, write,
Stab, stab, write,
A lil' pause to
Wipe out the blood,
Stab, stab, write.


Stab, stab, write,
Stab, stab, write,
Why do I fight?
That coffin is too tight.
Stab, stab, write.
Stab, stab, write.


Stab, stab, write,
Stab, stab, write,
Where are the lights?
I hear my thoughts, so quiet.
Stab, stab, write.
Stab, stab, write.

# Broken Toy

Ah, my darling baby boy!
Unfortunately mommy
Can not fix everything!
*-She does not know*
*How to fix*
*A broken heart.-*

# Self-Doubts

The more I write,
The bigger it gets!
Sometimes, I feel like
This pain in my chest
Is like the 3rd child
I'm trying to parent
And oh,
It always acts up!
All these tantrums of it,
I can't bear most of the time.
Now I ask myself,
What kind of a parent
Am I????

# Oh Boy

*"What's the worst that can happen?"*
You ask.
I chuckle nervously.
Boy, I will get hurt,
I will get burnt.
Yet,
You still have
No freakin' idea.

# Inner Monologues Of Mine

Hey heart,
I am wasted,
I am wrecked,
Gimme a break!


I am an unbalanced deck,
They have to check and double-check,
These ties they try after a trek,
Like a deadweight of a useless paycheque.


You grab my neck,
Line sweet sugar-coated peck,
-Here and there-
I ask myself, *the heck????*
My heart is a prosec,
This, I gonna admit,
I am a totalled car wreck
With the biggest hit
I ever take.

# Defining Love

On my jelly legs, I am not steady,
Why don't you kill me already?
I will never ever be ready,
But somehow, I am heady,
Why don't you kill me already?


My heart has always been petty,
Why don't you kill me already?
*"I will love you,"* said he, sweaty,
Oh boy, oh boy, I see a deep tragedy,
Why don't you kill me already?


All these thoughts, words, I have many,
Most of them are violent and deadly,
I sink deep down, this pain is too heavy,
These legs feel like unsteady kinda jelly,
Not sure how long they can carry,
Regrets, I hope not to have any!
In your ribcage, tuck me in and bury,


*Oh boy, oh boy,*
*Why don't you kill me already?*

# Ambrosia, Poison Of Choice

Your lips are heaven,
High on ambrosia, cursed.


Kicked out of heaven,
How dare I,
Feast on an angel?


*Oh boy, oh boy,*
*I am soooo high*
*On your sweet nectar,*
*Flowing*
*From*
*Your*
*Mouth,*
*Venomous.*

# Type Me In

I am a blank white paper,
Fill me in,
Type me in.
Let your fingers,
Create our truth,
Moving passionately
On the typewriter of yours,
Creating me and you.
Again.

# Matrix

I do not know what to feel,
Which side is up or down anymore.
I either fall down to your feet
Or rise so high above the crown you wear.
When I am down, at my weakness,
It is the matrix of tenderness,
That makes me stay,
For all these years,
For all these lifetimes.

# Silence Of Mind

This silence gets the best of me sometimes,
My mind sways to the edges without any balance,
All these words I write on the pale paper,
Naked walls and bare shelves,
Empty displays of my soul,
Controlled, cold and hollow.

# Mind Tricks Of Lovely Universe

Whenever I say, *"Girl, we need to move on now,*
*That ship had already sailed,"*
My playlist shuffles, I hear your husky voice,
Is it a coincidence or a sign?

# Dead In The Cage

This longing in my soul,
Seeking for its long-lost home
I breathe in, I breathe out,
I look around, I reach out.
My home, my long-lost love…
Oh, my empty nest..
My poor, stillborne heart...

# Disco

All these glimmers of hope and love
I see in your eyes,
Catches me off guard and knocks me down
Off of my feet.
Your smile is like mirrorball stars,
I am blinded from the start.

# Glory On My Skin

Morning glory unfolds on my skin,
Winter sun kisses every inch,
*"Relax baby, no more scorching,*
*Only enjoying each other."*

# Too High To Handle

High on my own blood and throbbing pain,
Watching the purulence seep out from my skin,
I am highly intoxicated of
The love wounds you gave to me.

# Fade

Lately, the dusty maze of my mind
Is missing all its borders,
Everything is so entangled,
What starts, what finishes?
Who are all these faces?
I look at the mirror,
It is all blank,
Then where am I?


I grasp to what I can remember,
Every memory I may recapture
Crumbles away,
I look at the blank mirror,
I am faceless,
My conscious is all broken,
It is fading faces.

# Siren Calls

Relax and fade into me,
I will keep you safe and warm,
Listen to the sound of my breathing,
Envision how I wash away the pain and tears.
Can't you hear me singing for you?
Take a step baby,
Be one with my ocean soul.

# Game Over

I do not care about who came before me,
We saw how it ended,
You, singing out all these bloody heartbreaks.
I want to be your end game,
The one who will wrap all your wounds,
Kiss these heartbreaks away,
Heal yourself along myself,
Knead your soul into mine.


*Boy, oh my boy,*
*You got it all wrong.*
*I aim to be your end game,*
*With me now,*
*Game over.*

# My Aurora

Winter child at heart,
That white blanket magic of snow,
That hot chocolate covered of your lips,
That flannel blanket you wrap around us,
My heart dances like aurora,
In your sky, shamelessly.

## Love/Hope

Fall in love with me,
I'll love you as much as I hope,
Fall in love with me.

# Lighthouse

She hid her light,
To blend in a dull crowd.
She tucked her heart in
A treasure chest,
Locked it in a closet.
To be a part of the society,
She hid her light,
*"Not far from view,"* said he,
Seeing the shine from afar.

# Art Master

You think I am cold and callus
For I do not cry and mourn behind my losses.


*Boy, oh boy,*
*I'd mastered the art of letting go*
*From a young age.*

# Holes In My Soul

Love thyself, the most important of my valuable goals
Sometimes it is hard, changed are the roles and controls,
Never forget, we all have various holes in our souls.

# Sibling Rivally

I'm your elder brother, listen to me,
You are always gonna be my little sister.
I had loved you when you were in mummy's tummy,
Put my small hands on the big tummy and tried to make
you kick back.
I will always love you, dear sister,
I will always be the rock for you to lean on.


Let's go places, because we can,
The world is our playground.
I will always keep an eye on you
Just like mummy did with me and you.


This string is mine, with all respects,
Love and loyalty,  our silly but endless sibling rivalry,
We thrive on teasing each other,
But nobody messes with my little sister!!!!

# Lucas

Layer by layer
Falls your clothing
Down on the floor.
You stand naked,
Baring yourself to me.
All these scars you took,
All these beauty marks on your skin,
I aim to memories,
Brand in my mind.


You are used to my silence,
This sly expression on my face.
You walk closer to me,
Making me wonder who is the prey,
Who is the hunter now.


You lick your lips,
My teeth draw blood from mine.
*Oh boy, oh boy,*
*I soooo see what I like,*
*All I can say is*
*Niceeeeee.*

# Eager

Anticipation
-I want you to touch me now-
 Kills me, waiting game.

# Artsy Craftsy

You ask, *"What is art?"*
Boy, my boy, it is like this
Firework emotions I get
Whenever I watch you
Lick me off your lips.
Gets me every time,
Dissolves all
The particles of my mind,
Then reassembles again,
Setting me free from all this pain,
Making me shine brighter.

# Play Me Out

Touch me here and there
Stroke all my tense guitar strings
My body aches, sing.

# White Magic

Cast a spell on me snow,
Make me either fall in love again,
Or simply out of love.

# The joke is on me

Whenever I think
You mean it
When you tell
You love me,
Universe screams and claps,
There is always a twist in the tale.

# Time and me

Can't wrap my head around time
Seconds pass in snail speed
I count the hours to bed
I look back and only 10 minutes passed??
Felt like ages!


Can't wrap my mind around time
Look now how they had grown up,
All these words I write,
All this love I am giving....
Feels like yesterday but years ago?


I really, really, really
Can't wrap my mind around time.

# Roulette

Loving you
Is a Russian roulette.
I never knew
If I would survive
Or have another round
Of this insanity.

# Peacock

Glorious peacock,
Spread your feathers wide for me,
Show off your glory.

# Hanging On The Wall

My pain is like all these floral decorations,
Dry, barely alive, always ignored,
Hang on a muted, dull wall.

# Turmoil

I wear my heart on a sleeve,
Yet, you still do not see what I feel,
What you do to me.


*Oh boy, oh boy,*
*You have no idea*
*About the turmoil I hide inside,*
*It is reflecting in my eyes.*

# Losing Game

I had lost my silly and irrational hope,
Clinging to the tiniest possibility
Of me and you,
Together,
Forgetting about the miles and oceans
Between us.


*Boy, oh boy,*
*I am not sure*
*If I had somehow,*
*Someway*
*Lost*
*A*
*Big*
*Chunk*
*Of*
*Myself*
*As well…*

# The Healer

Spreading love around,
Wanna heal each soul I see,
Duct-tape memories.

# Gazing Through You&Me

You press open-mouthed kisses
From my heart to my mouth.
You smile and my heart beats madly in overdrive,
You do not say the words,
But the way you hold my gaze
Makes me blush down to my core.


*Oh boy, my boy,*
*Oh well….Even I,*
*Do not have the correct*
*Word to express that.*

# Secluded Corner

My pain is a restless ocean,
Keeps caressing your beach of skin
For her own comfort.
You and me,
We fall into this blissful silence,
Watching the levitating moonlight
Playing peak-a-boo
In our secluded heaven.

# Titanic

Sinking into my bathtub,
Like a shipwreck I feel,
I have no place to store
All this pain and heartbreak
Aftermath of the flood of my tears,
Mingled with yours.

# Playing Mind Games

Wanna play with all this emotion,
Your fall will be your commotion,
I have always stated my devotion,
Oh boy, the plan is in motion.

# Obedience

I want to hear you say,
These three simple words,
Staring deep into my eyes,
Your lips swollen and wet
From my kissing.


*Oh boy, one of us has to say it:*
*I am yours,*
*To do as you please.*

# Magic Blanket

Be the snow of my soul,
Cover me in this magical blanket
Of yours.

# Cerulean

Wanna get lost in,
Cerulean eyes of yours.
Not blue not green,
Like the thin ice
We are standing.

# Pain

At first the denial slips from my lips,
I bite my lips in anger.
Anger turns into endless fury,
I want to destroy everything
On my way like a tornado.
Knowing I can't, destroy,
The acceptance sinks down slowly,
Accompanied by self-guilt.
I sit there mesmerized and hushed,
While the pain makes a happy tap dance
To be the one for ruling my world.

# Glass Heart

Running to your aid
Like a rescue mission I am,
Before you slip/trip, fall,
Break the glass of heart
You drag all around.

Memories Of Us
One Thousand Memories Of our death


Anxious
I put my head between my legs,
Rocking myself back and forth.
My focus slips, my gaze is all blurry,
I am unable to focus on anything,
You talk with me on and off,
I do not even hear your words
But you pull me back.

# Evaporating Of Mind

Time is slipping away,
Disoriented memories,
Forgotten conversations,
Scattered thoughts,
Dissolves into nothingness.


The best of me is lost,
Like a damn pair of glasses
I keep looking all around,
Forgetting they are on my head.


There lives a thief in my head,
Stealing moments, stealing love, light.
All I have is stolen memories,
Who will show the light in darkness now?


A shell of what I was,
It would be a lie to say
I'm still me,
I do not remember who I was,
I do not know who I am now.

Somebody I do not know
Tries to hold my wrinkled hand.
The vision of mind vanquished,
Talks to me in a soft, tender voice,
As if I am a baby in fear,
Unable to comprehend the world.


Baby...where did I put my baby?
Who was my baby?
Where did I leave these damn glasses?
Where am I, where am I?
Where is the light?